THE POWER OF
PLAY, PRAISE, AND
PURPOSE

THE POWER OF PLAY, PRAISE, AND PURPOSE

THE BEST KEPT SECRETS OF THRIVING ENTREPRENEURIAL COUPLES

KELLY CLEMENTS

Printed in the United States of America

LCN: 2017957009

ISBN Paperback: 978-1-54994046-0
ISBN eBook: 978-1-947368-30-9

Cover Design: Neslihan Yardimli
Interior Design: Ghislain Viau

Dedication of Gratitude

To David for the experience

To my sons, Will & Luke, for the motivation

***

*This book, nor it's lessons, are possible without
the work of others who have gone before me.*

*Specifically, my mentor, John, who opened doors and
lead the way into creating a business out of a calling.*

*For Dan Sullivan & Babs Smith, founders of Strategic
Coach. It was in your Chicago office where I collided head
first with my purpose. Not a day goes by that I am not
grateful for your pioneering spirits.*

*Also, Jon & Missy Butcher, whose relationship set the bar
for what's possible through a thriving love relationship.*

*Finally, for my parents, who gave a real life
example for how two ordinary people create and
sustain an extraordinary relationship.*

*And of course, so much love to my friends. Each of you
are NEXT LEVEL and your support, encouragement,
and own unique talents inspire me in every way.*

CONTENTS

Author's Story. ix

Introduction 1

Part One: The Storms of Entrepreneurial Relationships

Chapter 1 | Roles vs. Identity. .9

Chapter 2 | Strengths vs. Weakness 15

Chapter 3 | Reality vs. Expectations. 19

Part Two: The Secrets of Thriving Entrepreneurial Couples

Chapter 4 | The Power of Play. 27

Chapter 5 | The Power of Praise 41

Chapter 6 | The Power of Purpose. 55

The Launch Pad: It Takes Two Extraordinary People
    to Create One Extraordinary Relationship. 75

Additional Information:

    Renewing Yourself through Your Marriage. 81

    Entreprenewer Coaching Services 82

AUTHOR'S STORY

It was the relationship of my dreams with my own personal superman, David. He was a natural entrepreneur and exuded charisma and class. He had been in business for himself since 1983, when he was just fifteen years old. The son of a struggling immigrant, he began washing cars in his parents' driveway. He put himself through school at Indiana University, where he earned a business degree. As "luck" would have it, upon graduation, one of his customers handed him the keys to his airplane and said his "plane was starving for a good cleaning." David cleaned that airplane better than it ever had been cleaned before, which landed him in the headquarters of NetJets, an international company owned by Warren Buffett that serves as a timeshare for private jets. They were so impressed with David, they offered him an invitation to open up a location at any of their bases so he could detail their entire fleet. The rest, as they say, *took off* from there.

That opportunity led to many others, and soon he would have locations all over the world. He won cleaning contracts with many of the manufacturers who built these airplanes. He had, quite literally, changed the game in the industry. The passion he had for his work was undeniable, and to me, it was irresistible. Driven by vision and purpose, he was exactly what I desired in a partner.

I had been a consultant, coaching entrepreneurs for over a decade, when we began dating. In our relationship, we had freedom and flexibility. We had ideas and avenues to pursue them. We had vision and autonomy. With multiple residences, our own plane, and friends all over the world, the planet was our playground. Most important, we had a deep, meaningful connection. We were completely synchronized in the major areas of life. We missed each other when we were apart and revered one another when we were together. We were the weirdest people we knew, but together, we made sense. Stride for stride, we were indivisible. But there was an unperceived threat bubbling under the surface—one that would be revealed two years into our relationship.

"KEELLLLLYYYYY!" David's distressed voice wailed through the phone. Violent, heaving sobs replaced his usually strong, steady voice. His words were garbled in the pouring rain. Angry semi-trucks whizzing by in the background slammed on their horns. My mind's eye conjured up a gruesome scene. An avid cyclist, he had gone on a bike ride earlier that day to clear his head. With no coherent information, and the chaos building, I assumed he had been hit by a car. I pressed him for clear information so I could call 911. More desperate sobbing followed by F-bombs. Eventually, I would be able to distinguish some key words. "Bankruptcy." "Court." "Judge." More F-bombs. Inconsolable wailing. "Lawyers!" "Verdict." Sobbing. "Nothing!" "Lost. It. ALL!" Raging, visceral F-bomb. Click. Silence.

His business, his life's work, had just been vaporized in bankruptcy court. This wasn't an ordinary bankruptcy case. Nothing he did was *ordinary*. Everything was over the top, and this was no exception. This bankruptcy case would involve a competitor and, ultimately, entangle the entire private-aviation industry. It was high-profile and highly personal.

After eighteen months in and out of court, up against a mountain of lawyer's bills, personal allegations, traumatized team members, disappointed customers, and his devastated children, his life had come to a screeching halt! The judge had just issued her verdict and denied his motion to continue running his business. Everything was gone with a slam of the gavel. The territory he had covered during his fall was impressive. His meteoric rise was matched only by his devastating defeat.

Staying by his side as he was dragged through the mud was a no-brainer for me. He was my guy and we were planning to marry. Plus, this was exactly what I had asked for. After years of working with the entrepreneurial elite, I could think of nothing better than to marry a business owner. I knew the highs and the lows of business. More specifically, I knew the highs *matched* the lows. I knew his genius, and I knew his next chapter would make up for all that he had suffered during this season of loss. I knew this journey all too well after watching other business owners move through this kind of entrepreneurial pitfall. What I didn't know was the massive toll entrepreneurship had on the spouse or partner. I was about to find out!

In the months that followed the loss of his business, I would go on to lose *myself*. I'd lose myself in the assumed responsibility of saving him from his emotional torment. I'd lose myself in the cesspool of negativity, lack, anguish, and despair. I'd lose myself in the haunting, cold shadow of his failure. I'd lose myself in the overcrowded space of his one-man pity party.

My man lost his business to bankruptcy, and I lost my man to his defeat. I would go on to lose my health, my perspective, my hope, my shine, my dreams, and my sense of self. I lost my creativity and my vision. I lost my spark. I lost my way.

I was in a constant state of *output*. It was like letting out a long, slow breath, then pushing harder, in a constant state of exhale. Never finding an opportunity to stop and breathe in, I was evaporating. *But who was I to complain?* I hadn't just lost *my* life's work. I wasn't the one who'd gone through public humiliation. I wasn't the one who had lost the ability to provide for my family. *Suck it up, buttercup! You have no room to feel sorry for yourself.* Even if I were to complain, no one was there to listen. My partner was too consumed with his own suffering to be able to focus on mine.

That said, there was one thing I knew for sure: I had to stay strong. I knew a spouse or a partner could make or break a business. As much as we would like to believe the two can be compartmentalized, I've learned otherwise: a spouse plays an undeniable role in the success of a business, even if he or she has never set foot in the office.

What I didn't know, and what I was utterly unprepared for, was the experience of the spouse. I had only ever seen the entrepreneur's side of the journey. If being an entrepreneur is lonely, it can be even lonelier to be married to one. We don't have access to the peer-to-peer–centered mastermind groups, networks, coaches, books, blogs, and speakers, like entrepreneurs do. We hear fragmented stories from what makes it home from the office that day. We see the glaring computer screens in the middle of sleepless nights. We wonder if other parents in the school pickup line know what it's like to cover a $75,000 payroll each week. We hold it all together with the limited information we have, fearing the worst, hoping for the best.

Eventually, David would get a second chance at rebuilding his business. That would prove to be the easy part. Rediscovering myself would prove more difficult, and sadly, that cost us the opportunity to rebuild the relationship. The loss of his business and my self cost us our coveted relationship. But it wasn't lost in vain. It was through that loss that I had the breakthrough experience that so many entrepreneurial couples hold their marriage hostage to the state of the business. I learned that things have to contract before they expand. Most important, I learned that the spouse and the entrepreneur have equal ownership in the creation of an extraordinary relationship.

Through my own personal journey and my work with hundreds of entrepreneurial couples, I've learned the best-kept secret of all: **in order to create one extraordinary love relationship, we need two extraordinary people.**

INTRODUCTION

Entrepreneurship is a wild ride and it takes the right person to pull it off successfully. With over 90 percent of entrepreneurs failing once or more in business, it's no wonder the divorce rate for entrepreneurs is so high. The journey of entrepreneurship is wrought with extreme highs and lows. Add a spouse to the mix and you either have a secret weapon—or a recipe for disaster!

For a spouse, marrying into an entrepreneurial relationship can prove to be a tremendous blessing or a blasted curse. I used to say that a spouse can make or break a business. While that's still true, there's a more important truth: a business can make or break a spouse.

While the growth of a business owner may serve the business well, it can also threaten a marriage. When couples are not growing together, the gap of shared goals and dreams can swallow the relationship. Because a spouse plays such a crucial support role to the business owner, it is imperative to invest in the individual growth of the spouse as well as the entrepreneur. Most spouses struggle to find the line between support and self-care. Discovering how to effectively manage the impact of the business on the spouse and the relationship has proven to be a game changer.

The impact of a supportive spouse on a *business* in undeniable. The impact of a fulfilled spouse in a *relationship* is even greater. That's why the spouses must be championed, acknowledged, and encouraged to grow and care for themselves. To be healthy in all areas of personal life requires a journey of self-discovery to reconnect with one's highest and best self.

I've lived in the uncertain environment of the entrepreneurial households on both sides of the equation—as the entrepreneur *and* as the partner of one. I've learned from my mistakes and love lost. I've also coached many entrepreneurial couples through Strategic Coach, Lifebook, and my own business, The Entreprenewer, where I recognized they were all experiencing similar issues, not only in the business, but in the situation at home.

Due to the constant demands of the business and family, couples are often left feeling deflated, overwhelmed, and underserved. They're in chronic reaction mode. The entrepreneur is hyper-focused on maximizing their potential in the business. The spouse is caught up in the inertia of everyone else's goals and dreams. They aren't pursuing their own passion and growth anymore. In essence, both parties are being squeezed out of the relationship. They have forgotten the three most enjoyable parts of life and relationships: the power of play, the power of praise, and the power of purpose.

My intention for this is a book is to empower entrepreneurial couples to grow TOGETHER through the powers of play, praise, and purpose. Harnessing these powers will reveal that it takes TWO extraordinary people to create ONE extraordinary relationship. In discussing the concepts, I will often refer to entrepreneurial relationships in a generalized way, referring to the entrepreneur as "he" and the spouse as "she"—but the challenges can be just as hard, if not harder, when the woman is the entrepreneur in the relationship. The same is true for same-sex couples of either gender. These principles are boiled down to "entrepreneurship + the human experience," and transcend stereotypes and gender roles.

To create a healthy, vibrant relationship, the three most crucial strategies involve infusing your relationship with prolific amounts of play, praise, and purpose. In the next section, we'll address why entrepreneurs and their spouses need to match the quality of their free time to that of their work time. We'll explore how they can bring greater awareness to their opportunities to affirm versus accuse, and identify the need to align their long-term visions so there's purpose in both their lives, as well purpose for their relationship. In short, entrepreneurial households require plentiful play, potent praise, and powerful purpose.

PART ONE

THE STORMS OF ENTREPRENEURIAL RELATIONSHIPS

B efore we explore the solution, we must fully recognize the problem. If we don't understand what's hurting us, we can't maximize what helps us.

Entrepreneurship offers a unique dynamic to a love relationship. Somehow, the business becomes a third party in the relationship. It can become the source of our identity and the catalyst for the health (or lack thereof) of our relationship. It becomes the governing body of how well we "show up" for our spouse. It is crucial for us to reclaim our love relationship from the grip of our business if we are to truly step into our power as a couple.

Chapter 1

ROLES VS. IDENTITY

Identity loss: It doesn't take a crisis.

We give business owners a lot of flack for tying their identity so tightly to their business. Their self-worth becomes inextricably linked to their net worth. What has so far gone unnoticed is how strongly the spouse ties her identity to the business owner. The business now becomes the foundation of the relationship. But we overlook the crucial piece in which we acknowledge that the love relationship is actually the bedrock of a fulfilling life *and* the health of the business.

Remember, in order to create one extraordinary love relationship, we need two extraordinary people—not one extraordinary business. We need two people who are actively paying attention to their needs and desires. We need two people who are committed to shared growth and mutual support. By nature, and by trade, entrepreneurs are hard-wired for growth. They seek peak experiences and are always looking for an edge. Many times, the result of this quest for hyper-growth leaves thrashing chaos in its wake. The spouse is left to hold the rest of the couple's lives together. Keeping life on the rails becomes a full-time job, and it's in this abyss that we completely lose sight of ourselves.

Crisis and Complacency
Are Equal-Opportunity Destroyers

It was the most important workshop I had facilitated to date. A group of twelve well-respected, influential entrepreneurs and their spouses were scouting the program for potential distribution opportunities. The growth potential of this one workshop was exponential. The couples had flown to Chicago for a private, four-day coaching session. All the business-owners were men in their thirties to mid-sixties, and all were game-changers in their respective industries. They were looking for that next edge; only this time, they were bringing their spouses. I couldn't WAIT to work with these couples! I knew many of the business owners from previous coaching programs and I understood how much they counted on their spouses. After my experience with David, I now had a special place in my heart for the role the spouse plays. These women were committed to being there with their husbands and stepping into their own power. In a sense, it was their time to shine. For four days, the couples would be nestled in an elegant loft, lovingly called the "Chocolate Cocoon," thanks to its rich, two-story, brown-suede–covered walls. The space was ultra-luxurious and specifically designed to foster big thinking. I was tasked with challenging the couples to think about their lives, set goals, and break barriers. For many of the spouses, this was the first time they had taken time to actively think about what they wanted. The first day was a breeze, with lots of lively discussions as new possibilities began to emerge.

On the second day, something unexpected and transformative happened. The participants were sprawled out across oversized sofas and had just finished a journaling exercise. I reconvened the group and invited them to gather in the center of the space for a group discussion.

With powerful, dynamic dialogue so far, I was looking forward to hearing new breakthroughs. But as they made their way to the circle, it was quiet. The group's energy level had shifted dramatically. The mood was now quite somber and they were disengaged, avoiding eye contact and shifting in their seats. Despite my best engagement strategies, no one was willing to share. It was getting very awkward, very fast.

Acknowledging the tension in the room, I said, "Time out. What's going on?" There was silence. "I can wait," I gently offered.

Suddenly, Jamie, one of the spouses in her early forties, spoke. As she began, she gently cleared her throat and tucked a piece of her blond hair behind her ear. Her natural sophistication and intelligence were on full display.

She said, "Kelly, I just don't know how to do this. I had an executive career before I stayed home with our kids. I used to set goals at work, but I just don't know how to think about *my* life anymore. And quite frankly, I don't even feel like it matters. I don't feel like I get a vote, because I'm so busy just keeping life *together*."

I knew her feeling all too well, but it didn't seem right. Her husband's financial business was thriving and they had never experienced the type of crisis David and I had gone through. How had she lost herself in what, from the outside, seemed like a perfect life?

As I looked around the room, the other spouses were either nodding in agreement or holding back tears. Jamie had struck a nerve. What followed was the most vulnerable, insightful conversation the group would have. One woman shared that she was scared to look inside so deeply because she feared she wouldn't find anything.

"What if there really is nothing left?" another spouse added. "Or worse, what if I find it and it doesn't fit in our life?"

The most profound share would come from Marcy. Through tears and with a shaky voice, she turned to her husband: "It's like you shine so bright, but sometimes it feels like you're sucking out all of my oxygen."

Ouch! I needed to turn this around—and fast. The weekend was about empowerment, not resentment. The resentment was surfacing as the spouses stood face-to-face with their lack of personal identity. In that moment, the goal of the workshop shifted from "landing the deal" to helping the spouses rediscover their identity and their *purpose.*

I *knew* I was their girl. I would spend the balance of that workshop helping the spouses reclaim their senses of self. It was now my mission to balance the scales of passion and purpose for these couples. Mission accomplished! By the end of that workshop, two women chose to reenter the workforce, one requested a leadership role at her church, one joined her husband's business, and one woman and her husband started a "juice truck" as a hobby business. The other women accepted the position of "CHO"—Chief Household Officer.

Rachel, a mother of ten, said it best: "Wealth lies in the difference between what we make and what we spend. If he's responsible for making it for the family, I'm responsible for keeping it in the family. That breakthrough alone helps me realize I really am on equal financial footing with my husband." Amen, sister!

Watching the spouses dig deep into finding their purpose exposed the loss of identity in the business owner. The elephant in the room became the entrepreneurs; formerly full of advice, they were now being called to task on defining their own identities, independent from the business. The prime example was Andre, a young Silicon Valley phenom who had sold his business and retired at thirty-two. The sale of his dot-com resulted in a windfall—which landed him in a bed with the covers over his head and in a sea of depression. Being removed from his platform left him completely devoid of any sense of self-worth. He used the breakthroughs of the spouses to inform his pursuit of what the next chapter of his life would be. Honoring his unique gifts and talents and how they could be used outside of the business inspired an opportunity to incubate up-and-coming entrepreneurs with mission-driven goals.

When the workshop ended on the fourth day, we had a green light from every couple in the room. Chapter 6, The Power of Purpose, will illustrate the strategies that took the workshop, and the participants' marriages, to the next level.

Chapter 2

STRENGTHS VS. WEAKNESS

*Our greatest strength can
also be our greatest weakness.*

B ryan was the quintessential entrepreneur. He was wildly innovative, wizard smart, interesting, confident, and driven. He effortlessly commanded respect and could light up any room. All who came into his orbit were instantly drawn to him. He spoke with such passion and conviction about his work that he effortlessly enrolled others in his vision—and those qualities had scored him the woman of his dreams, Jessica.

When they'd met, Bryan had been a budding entre-preneur. He'd had some lukewarm success at various entrepreneurial ventures, but he knew that with a woman like Jessica by his side, he'd be "bulletproof." Of course, he was right. Jessica saw his budding genius and knew that, with a little support, they could build a tremendous life together. They shared a passion for health and fitness, and, together, they would turn that passion into profit. They started their own line of fitness products and worked hard to get them to the mass markets. As the business took off, it created leverage for them to start a family. Jessica opted to stay home and focus on their growing family, while Bryan would continue promoting their products.

Their evolving partnership grew deeper, and he was in awe as he watched Jessica with their new child. She was a natural—just as she had been in the business. Knowing the sacrifice Jessica had made to her professional life to stay home with their daughter inspired Bryan like never before. He made a vow to himself that he would never let either of these miraculous creatures go without what they wanted or needed.

With renewed passion and a turbocharged vision, Bryan went to work. A few years later, their line of products reached its tipping point and was soon found in every major retailer in North America. It started generating massive publicity and Bryan was quickly becoming the face of the business.

Every month, he was gaining hundreds of new followers on social media. He would excitedly share stories with

Jessica about all the influencers who were promoting and retweeting him. He was being featured on celebrity blogs and podcasts. He was invited to speak at conferences and seminars. He was having the time of his life!

The growing fan base was no surprise to Jessica. She had seen the potential in Bryan a decade ago, before he was "Bryan." But she wondered, *Why is all of this new attention from strangers suddenly more exciting than my encouragement of him?* The reason: somewhere along the way, she had stopped giving him that support and inspiration.

With a child in the mix, his innovation started feeling like chaos to Jessica. His passion and drive started feeling like mania. What had seemed "wizard smart" before now seemed wildly out of touch. His conviction felt like stubbornness, and his confidence, quite frankly, had become arrogance. His ability to light up any room often left Jessica and their daughter at home in his shadow.

What's worse, all his success at work was constantly overshadowing the milestones she was reaching at home with their child. She had opted out of the business to focus on what was, in her opinion, a more important pursuit. *So why is he the one getting all the accolades?* she wondered. *Is a new line of vitamins suddenly more noteworthy than our daughter's first word—which, by the way, was "dada"?*

In Bryan's mind, Jessica's lack of excitement for his success could only be explained by her "obsession" with their child. Suddenly, what he'd so ardently admired about Jessica just a few years prior was now a source of conflict. What he had once described as "her natural ability to mother," he now saw as "helicopter parenting." While Jessica was once so confident as a parent, now she was second-guessing everything as a result of Bryan's criticism.

Herein lies the problem: Their strengths were now seen as weaknesses. What had initially attracted them, now repelled them. The compliments had been replaced by complaints. That can expose an even bigger issue involving how women crave security and men seek significance. Entrepreneurship offers a massive amount of significance for the entrepreneur but very little security for the spouse. The business becomes a major asset for one and a major liability for the other. The scales tip in the business owner's favor. As a result, the relationship suffers because it has become one-dimensional. This is a contributing factor to why a spouse can become insecure, which is a trigger for lodging stronger complaints. If we are still getting our identity from the business owner, the deficit we feel can become, in our mind, the fault of the business owner. Chapter 5, The Power of Praise, will help instill the strategies *both* partners can use to create the powerful relationship of their dreams.

Chapter 3

REALITY VS. EXPECTATIONS

All conflict lies in the gap
between expectation and reality.

Another common problem that occurs between entre-preneurs and their spouses lies in the gap between expectation and reality. Entrepreneurs are creative thinkers, visionaries, and pioneers. They see potential and big opportunity *everywhere.* The sky's the limit and obstacles are mere gut checks on the road to global domination. Part of their appeal is the way they enroll everyone around them in their vision. The spouse is on-boarded with euphoric promises: "This will change the world!" "All our problems are solved!" "We'll finally get that beach house we've always wanted!" "We'll retire by the age of forty!" The spouse is highly engaged, throwing her support behind the business. The expectation has been set.

As the business grows, a different reality sets in: We're working all day, every day. We're borrowing money from family and friends. And the business is taking more time and resources than anyone expected.

It is in this space of mismanaged expectations that conflict is born. All disappointment lies in the gap between expectations and reality. The widening breach between what was promised and what is delivered can quickly turn into marital dissent.

One place where expectations are wildly out of whack for entrepreneurs is in the area of work-life balance. Our brains are *always* on, and being in chronic work mode has a cost—not only to our productivity at work and personal health, but also to the potential of our love relationship. We often miss the early warning signs that a disconnect from our spouse has occurred. When the business requires so much of our attention, it's easy to blame the business for our failing relationship. But what if there's another culprit at play here?

When I started working at an entrepreneurial coaching company called Strategic Coach, I noticed a startling truth. Entrepreneurs were flying in from all over the world to achieve balance through a concept of "Free Days." After all, the marketing tagline was, "Work Less. Make More." Dan Sullivan, the company's founder, famously enjoys 250 free days per year while consistently growing his business! Free days are, by definition, twenty-four hours, midnight to midnight, with NO work-related activities: no office check-ins, no e-mail messages, no reading business publications, nothing. It's an entire day to focus on rejuvenation and being something other than an entrepreneur. The reason is clear: Free Days are a prerequisite to success, not a reward for it. Business owners registered for the program in droves to learn how to experience these elusive free days while growing their businesses.

The concept was so paramount that it was the first lesson taught in this three-year program. The participants would have an entire quarter to implement these Free Days before they came back for their second workshop. At the start of the second workshop, we always began with a check-in on how the first quarter of Free Days went.

Without fail, we heard reports of Free Days gone wrong. It was too easy to assume that our invasive smartphones were to blame. Yes, with constant access to anyone, anywhere, the concept of "time away" was becoming more difficult to attain—but with a little probing, we discovered the truth.

For the entrepreneurs, Free Days just weren't *fun*. Clients would share some major "first-world" problems like, "It was really hard to stay engaged at the Little League game because it just wasn't that exciting." Some reported that while they did take twenty-four hours away from the business, those hours were spent carpooling, working on home-repair projects, going to doctor's appointments, etc. Others said that their spouses complained that they never got a Free Day off from their household responsibilities. So, instead of an enjoyable Free Day, they got a "honey, do" list and watched their spouses take some much-needed time off—without them.

The sentiment for each of these experiences was the same: "Free Days are a nice concept, but I'd rather be at work; it's more fun!" Entrepreneurship is fueled by adrenaline. There's a constant rush, and trying to take that drive out of a business owner is like trying to remove the German from a Mercedes. It's not going to happen.

You can imagine the conflict this creates for a spouse who is also craving high-quality free time. Often, entrepreneurs don't recognize that the spouse needs this coveted time off just as much. A classic example of this comes from Dr. Evan and his wife, Christine. On a video-coaching call with them, I asked how often they travel together. Dr. Evan was quick to explain that they travel all the time. They had just gotten back from Colorado together, and he went on to tell me about the great trip to Hawaii they had also enjoyed. Christine patiently listened to him talk about all the great places they had gone before she finally chimed in.

"Honey, Colorado was for a work conference. And so was Hawaii . . . and you went to that conference alone! I haven't been on a vacation in over a year and a half!"

Dr. Evan's jaw hit the floor as he came to this realization. No wonder they had been feeling disconnected! His high-quality free time had put the extra household burden on Christine. As he was recharging, she was depleting.

In Chapter 4, The Power of Play, we'll learn how to amp up your free time so that time at home is more invigorating than time at work. We'll throw the "work-life balance" myth out the window and get to work on more PLAY to create the relationship we desire!

* * *

The storms we've just described, while common in all relationships, are amplified in entrepreneurial relationships. If we're not careful, the lack of play, praise, and purpose will quickly erode our sense of self as well as our love relationship. So now that we've covered the problem, let's jump into the solution! The secrets shared in this book will help underscore the three best practices of extraordinary love relationships.

These practices transcend the "communication is key" advice that we're used to. They will dramatically intensify the connection, intimacy, and enjoyment you experience with the true love of your life: your spouse. Mastering the powers of play, praise, and purpose will turbocharge your love relationship. Grab your partner, and let's jump in!

PART TWO

THE SECRETS OF THRIVING ENTREPRENEURIAL COUPLES

Chapter 4

THE POWER OF PLAY

Time away from work is good,
but it's the power of play that truly rejuvenates
and builds sustainability in marriage and business.

Yes! It's time to talk about the fun stuff: PLAY! I'm super-passionate about play; in fact, I even have my degree in it! That's right, I have a bachelor of science in recreation. My passion for play is evident in all areas of my life, especially in my coaching. I use the "power of play" to reconnect spouses to how and why they fell in love in the first place. When I'm coaching a group workshop or working with a new client, one of the first questions I ask is, "How did you meet and when did you know your partner was *the one?*" The answers are almost always rooted in play, and that gives me crucial insight into how to get the couple back to basics when challenges arise.

My favorite couple that illustrates this is Katie and Larry, whose marriage began to suffer when they stopped engaging in the passion and fun that had brought them together.

By trade, Katie is a designer and Larry is a builder. In lifestyle, these two couldn't be more different from each other: think "heiress debutant" meets "rocker bad boy." In a hundred years, I would never have paired up these two—until I first heard them talk about their dating days. Katie lit up when she remembered how much bigger her world became with Larry, who has a passion for racing cars. She was exposed to a new, tight-knit community in the racing world. She brought appetizers to share with the other wives and girlfriends at the racing events, and seeing Larry in his element made him even more attractive to her. Katie loved watching him in his race car, conquering his dreams.

The slow fade began a couple of years after the wedding. Katie stopped going out to Larry's races and became reacquainted with her old hobbies of yoga and antiquing. In her mind, she was being supportive, because she was always encouraging Larry and never complained about his absence when he returned from a race weekend. Larry, on the other hand, was gutted. Races just weren't the same without his girl cheering him on from the stands.

What was even more detrimental was that Katie stopped seeing Larry in that badass light she adored so much. Without watching her guy in his element, she only saw the "builder" version of Larry, who could seem angry, burnt-out, and tiresome. Katie had made a good move by pursuing her own passions, but where she and Larry both fell short was in the area of sharing in each other's enjoyment; they had stopped playing *together*. When Katie sees Larry fully engaged and alive in his passion for racing cars, she remembers why she chose him as a partner. It is via play that our greatest strengths are revealed. Play diffuses unnecessary tension and reflects our highest connection in relationships. It helps to heal the damaged inner child that tends to cause so many problems in a love relationship.

As entrepreneurs, we can become so enthralled with work that we stop playing altogether. We use excuses like, "my work is my hobby" or "I love work so much, it doesn't feel like work!" When this mantra is adopted, entrepreneurial tendencies seep into the home—hence the lack of balance. You'll know this has happened when you see these signs:

1) **The spouse starts to feel like an employee.** Spouses often share with me that they can feel more like an employee than a spouse. "He's so good at delegating at the office, that he won't do ANYTHING at home unless he wants to do it." This comes across as disengagement at home AND it compounds the workload of the spouse—both of which prevent opportunities to play together.

2) **The business gets the best of him while his spouse gets the rest of him**. Coming home after a long day, severely depleted, on a constant basis robs the spouse of the emotional connection she craves to create and sustain a powerful love relationship.

3) **All of the family's travel plans revolve around business trips and conferences.** This can lead the spouse to stop dreaming for herself, because she gets the sense it's just her job to keep up with the inertia of the business.

For all of these tendencies, we look to an "f-word" for relief: "flow."

Flow and Play are Equal Opportunity Restorers

If you live with an entrepreneur, you've probably heard the term "flow" or "flow state" before. These terms refer to the zone that entrepreneurs get into when they are working in the sweet spot of their business. It's in "the zone" where time stands still and everything else seems to fade away. During flow states, superior breakthroughs "flow" through the business owner with very little effort and yield extraordinary results. Concepts of time and space disappear and a euphoric mental state is achieved.

In his book *The Rise of Superman: Decoding the Science of Ultimate Human Performance*, author, journalist, and entrepreneur Steven Kotler has written about the neuro-chemical changes during flow states that strengthen motivation, creativity, and learning. "The brain produces a giant cascade of neurochemistry. You get norepinephrine, dopamine, anandamide, serotonin, and endorphins. All five of these are performance-enhancing neurochemicals," said Kotler in the publication "Big Think." Each of these amplifies intellectual and cognitive performance.

Basically, we're talking about a euphoric cocktail of fulfillment and productivity. This is precisely the reason entrepreneurs have such a hard time disconnecting from their work. Work is where they get their fix. Achieving flow can be addictive for all the right reasons. However, that hit of flow often results in addiction, just like any other drug. We call this addiction "workaholism."

Entrepreneurs aren't the only ones who experience flow. Artists and athletes achieve flow states as well. Do you see a common thread here? Dancers, musicians, artists, basketball players, football players, etc.—they are out *playing* for a living, and they are the ones who most often experience flow. To help balance the work-life scales, your best strategy is to incorporate the same sense of euphoria into your personal life. This is best achieved through play. When you consider *play*, the goal is to achieve "carefree timelessness"— a state in which you lose track of time and the distracting roles and responsibilities of your day-to-day life. In play, you reconnect with your partner and engage in pleasurable activities that you both enjoy. This puts you into a shared zone of euphoria together and fosters a healthy environment to build sustainable and growing love.

For spouses, this can seem like a pipe dream. The good news is, you're about to learn the delegation strategies successful entrepreneurs use to grow their business, and use them to grow in your life. You'll need to shed the activities that drain you to make room for ones that will help you achieve flow. In order to make room for the life you'll love, you'll need to let go of the things that no longer serve you.

Start focusing on doing more of the activities you enjoy and fewer of the activities that exhaust and deplete you. You can find a copy of this exercise on my website: www.playpraiseandpurpose.com. In a nutshell, I'll have you list all the things you are responsible for on a daily, weekly, monthly, quarterly, and annual basis. What are the activities on your list that you absolutely dread? How about the things that you simply tolerate because no one else will do them? As those activities come to mind, I want you to figure out how to get rid of them. This can mean assigning them to someone else or deleting them entirely from your calendar. As you consider these activities, be careful of the tendency to "should" on yourself. Often, when it comes time for spouses to delegate, a degree of guilt takes over. "My partner works so hard in the business, I really *should* be available to do more of this tedious stuff." Maybe, but my experience as a business consultant and coach tells me that entrepreneurs are better served by a happy, fulfilled spouse than one who is burnt out and trying to give from the proverbial "empty cup." More important, the spouse has the opportunity to discover the line between support and self-care. Clearing some draining activities from your agenda creates space for you to pursue more engaging, fulfilling activities. This is precisely where you will create time and energy for more play with your partner.

I encourage you to think of your play life as a three-legged race. You and your partner should have one or two personal hobbies that you enjoy separately, but the majority of your recreational time should be spent together. Maybe that involves taking turns participating in each other's hobbies, or perhaps it means finding a shared interest you both enjoy. For men, in particular, it's incredibly important to spend recreational time together. In fact, many men would rank recreation second only to sex when they define their ideal relationship.

Prep, Play, Produce: The Rhythm of Work and Play

As entrepreneurs, we are uniquely positioned to maximize play by enjoying the freedom our entrepreneurial path provides. Remember, we work extra hard, so we have to play extra hard to replenish energy spent on the business.

It's time to get back to the reason you chose this crazy path and start cashing in on personal enjoyment. **Your free leisure time is a depreciating asset.** The longer you wait to cash in, the less enjoyable it is. Use it now, while your kids are young; they'll cherish the memories long after you're gone. Use it now, while your spouse still craves time with you; she'll appreciate you even more. Use it now, while your mind and body are healthy and able; it'll keep both active and vigorous.

Just like we need systems, processes, and procedures in our business, we require them for our play as well. I suggest implementing a preparation strategy to ensure you keep play as a priority. Preparing for play will maximize your play and ensure you are enjoying high-quality free time with your spouse.

During this time, you'll ensure all the necessary logistics are taken care of. When preparing for play days, think of everything you will need: Childcare? Carpool assistance? Reservations? Equipment rental? Special clothing? Spend prep days getting everything ready to pull off play so you won't get bogged down in the mechanics on the play day. On the actual play day, you should aim to wake up in a state of carefree timelessness, confident that all the details have been addressed so you can take life at your own pace. This day is exclusively devoted to enjoyment. Perhaps it's a leisurely morning before an afternoon hike. Or maybe it's an early spin class before an afternoon of antiquing. **The activity is irrelevant; the goal is shared enjoyment.**

One crucial conversation to have as a couple concerning play days is a discussion about pace. Play days can mean many things to many people, but they tend to go off the rails when individuals have different opinions on the pace of the day. Some crave a calm, leisurely pace with no set agenda. Others crave high-octane, sensory-rich experiences. Neither is right or wrong, but the couple should make sure the expectation is set beforehand. If you and your partner have opposing views, take turns experiencing each other's preference. Avoid the costly mistake of spending too much free time separately. Remember, the key to having a deeper connection and more to talk about is experiencing life with and through one another. Embracing your differences as an asset will deepen your connection and your own personal development.

Play in Action

The frequency of play in our life boils down to the frequency of play in each day. Every day, regardless of the *type* of day it is, should have some element of play in it. The following snapshot will help set a gauge for how to integrate more play into your life.

Daily: Each day, when both the entrepreneur and spouse first get home, connecting with each other for fifteen seconds can change the game. Yes, *seconds*. That's all it takes. If you want to be really specific, start that interlude with a six-second hug. Research has shown that it only takes six seconds of an embrace to release oxytocin, the love hormone. You've both had long, hard days and when these two worlds collide, it can make for some tense moments. As soon as your partner walks in the door, you'll need a pattern interrupt, a break from the routine with something new. As soon as you or she walks through the door, seek one another. It takes fifteen seconds to stand face-to-face, kiss, assess each other's emotion, and realign as a united front. A devoted fifteen seconds each day after work will start to change the tone of your relationship. Bonus points if you carve out fifteen minutes to sit and have a glass of wine or take a walk together every day!

Weekly: Date night. *Every* week. Every. Single. Week. Even when you don't like each other, and especially when you don't feel like it. My personal trainer's voice haunts me in these moments. Every time I'm tired and don't feel like doing another rep, she gently reminds me, "This is where we make our changes." She's right. The exact moment you lose the desire or the perceived need for date night is the same moment you need to double down on your dates. Those moments are the gateway to either a more powerful relationship, or a further disconnect. The power is in the play.

My colleagues in Massachusetts, Drs. Stephen and Camilla Franson, have an awesome strategy for this. Upon noticing that conversations about kids and logistics were dominating their date-nights, they implemented "Coffee Breaks." Coffee Breaks are weekly meetings they have with each other, typically on a Sunday, about managing logistics. Each week, they get out their calendars: work, school, appointments, extra-curricular activities, and they consolidate. They spend a *power hour* aligning their views on the week ahead, and deciding who needs to be where, when. They also use this time to clean up any messes in their own relationship. Dedicating time to being organized clears the way for them to focus on happier pursuits on their weekly date night.

Monthly: Hotel date night. This will quickly become one of your favorite nights! Let's face it; hotel sex is the best sex! It's a chance to focus exclusively on this crucial piece of our marriage. It's an unbridled opportunity to pay attention to each other without the threat of waking the kids or trying to turn a blind eye to the laundry hanging over that chair in the bedroom. It removes the excuse of needing to do dishes or pay bills that our households so conveniently present. There's also something about the effort and foresight that goes into hotel date night. Spending time packing and preparing for a night away offers us a chance to spice things up by including items that may not otherwise appear in our repertoire. Additionally, getting out of the house together at least once a month offers major leverage in avoiding, or escaping, ruts. It's a pattern interrupt of the status quo. It's a golden opportunity to be cared for as a couple, order room service, book a spa appointment together, and have someone else make the beds. This ritual will unleash some of your most playful indulgences!

Quarterly: Weekend getaway. For the same reasons listed above, a weekend getaway four times a year presents a unique opportunity to grow deeper as a couple. Getting out of our community and visiting other places helps us to keep things in perspective. It adds dimension and richness that other pursuits just don't deliver. Travel, when done right, changes us. What a gift it is to share those unique experiences with each other!

Annual: Full-week getaway. If you have young kids, this can be challenging. In fact, lack of childcare is *the* biggest obstacle most couples face in executing on this crucial task—or in spending any time alone together, for that matter. Ensuring your kids are not only cared for, but also entertained, will allow these experiences to be even more enjoyable. Consider asking another family to swap weeks with you so you can take turns getting away. Or find an overnight camp that will ensure the kids don't even know you're gone.

Once we get back to that carefree place of enjoying each other, we can see each other's strengths again. Through play, we get back to where we can see our spouse's qualities as strengths and recognize the things that we appreciate in him or her. That way, we can have more of those good, healthy feelings and qualities, as opposed to the logistics and obligations that can stifle a relationship. Couples that play together, stay together. Play well, and play often!

To create your personalized action plan, visit:
www.playpraiseandpurpose.com

Chapter 5

THE POWER OF PRAISE

What we appreciate, appreciates.

For a man, one of the most powerful forces in the world is a woman's love. A well-loved man can and will move mountains for his love. The only thing stronger than a woman's love is her rejection. If a woman's love can make a man, a woman's rejection will break him.

As with all married couples, what initially attracts us to our spouse can quickly become the very things that frustrate us about him or her. It's the classic case of our greatest strengths turning into our greatest weaknesses. However, in entrepreneurial couples, this is magnified because entrepreneurs tend to have a more dynamic spectrum of talents and gifts. What makes us successful in business can be a real challenge to manage at home.

In fact, did you know that from a psychological perspective, quite a large number of entrepreneurs are similar to psychopaths? It's true! Entrepreneurs have just found better ways to channel all that mania.

A 2016 study by forensic psychologist Nathan Brooks of Bond University found that 21 percent of CEOs have the same psychological profiles as psychopaths.[1] However, in *The Wisdom of Psychopaths*, Dr. Kevin Dutton describes how the psychopathic traits that we ordinarily associate as negative actually manifest as positive and powerful attributes in some of the greatest historical figures and political leaders of our time.[2] The 21 percent of CEOs who are "successful psychopaths" adopt traits such as fearlessness, confidence, ruthlessness, charisma, and focus, and find ways to productively channel them into business.

These studies illustrate how a character trait can be viewed as a strength or a weakness, depending on its context and how it is expressed—*and perceived*. You can view the very same qualities in your partner as either powerful strengths

---

1 Australian Psychological Society, "Corporate Psychopaths Common and Can Wreak Havoc in Business, Research Says," press release, September 13, 2016, https://www.psychology.org.au/news/media_releases/13September2016/Brooks.

2 Kevin Dutton, *The Wisdom of Psychopaths: What Saints, Spies, and Serial Killers Can Teach Us About Success* (New York: Farrar, Straus and Giroux, 2012), 11.

or detrimental weaknesses, depending on your perspective and what you cultivate through praise or criticism.

Let's look at the qualities that most entrepreneurs share: they're confident, resilient, independent, driven, innovative, and have an eye for excellence. These qualities are strengths needed to build a successful business. However, when pressure gets turned up or there is a loss of control, these very same qualities can show up as arrogance, stubbornness, tyranny, mania, eccentricity, and perfectionism. Understanding the triggers that flip a strength into a weakness can help to us foster a relationship focused on strengths and praise, not weakness and criticism.

Another factor that is not openly shared is that most entrepreneurs constantly doubt that they are truly good enough. They may look poised and confident from the outside, but inside, they are battling feelings of insecurity. The moment our spouse validates those thoughts through criticism, we lose even more hope. Conversely, being affirmed by our spouse can quiet those unruly fear patterns.

An entrepreneur's concept of praise is an area in which his strengths can work against him. Entrepreneurs are wired to see possibility. They often see potential others cannot see. Because they can see potential so easily in others, they are quick to offer guidance and suggestions, even if unsolicited. In the absence of praise, these suggestions can seem like criticism. It is essential to see and appreciate the good, not just the potential.

Criticism is fine; we all have times in our relationship when criticism is necessary. However, when we criticize more than compliment, we devalue our relationship with every passing comment. It's important to recognize our partner's strengths, because what we appreciate, appreciates. When it gets dark, it's easy to think the world is against us. It's easy to think we're a terrible failure. And as we know, it can get really dark on the journey of any relationship. Add entrepreneurship to the mix, and it can become even darker.

Praise is about elevating you and your spouse to a level where you really believe in each other. It's not based on hollow compliments—saying nice things just for the sake of saying them—but rather, on the idea of truly believing in someone. It's truly *seeing* and *being seen*. The definition of intimacy is *"Into me you see."* Intentionally seeing the best in our partners turns praise into an aphrodisiac.

We Expand to the Space We're Given

Have you ever noticed that the most unified couples are the ones who consistently show appreciation for each other? If there's anything they get right, it's the ability to genuinely praise one another. It's not because their partners are more perfect than ours; it's because they choose to see the good. They are not complaining about their spouses or the confines of their marriage for entertainment value. They're not seeking the pity of others for the "tough road" they have to traverse in their marriage. They're shining the light, together, on the power of their partnership.

I know a couple is bulletproof when I hear statements like, "I couldn't do this without my spouse," "He believed in me before I believed in myself," and "She's my biggest inspiration, my biggest fan." These entrepreneurs set high expectations for their spouses, and guess what? The spouses rise to meet those expectations. When others see the most extraordinary traits in us, we feel a level of connection and intimacy unlike any other. We rise to meet those high expectations when they are set through praise, not constant reminders that we are falling short.

Even when we criticize in a joking manner, it cuts deep. It not only hurts our partner, but it also diminishes our own positive feelings for him or her. After leading a webinar on this topic, I received an email from a participant who said, "You're right; we bash our husbands like it's a sport. My girlfriends and I are always complaining about how our men fall short. They're all pretty successful, but we're 'joking' about stupid stuff, and it affects the way I feel that night when I'm sitting next to my husband: irritated about things that don't really matter."

Men can feel that condemnation, and when they are chronically criticized, they will respond accordingly. In other words, when we hold low expectations of them and are heavy on the criticism, they shut down and prove us right. Conversely, when they feel that we hold them in high esteem and see their greatness, they will rise to meet those expectations and confirm our estimation of them every single time.

Your attitude and regard for your spouse has the power to transform him or her on a cellular level. If he's never enough for you and you're consistently disappointed, his contributions will continue to dwindle. But if you view him as a super hero, he will don his cape. If you see her for all that she already is, and not just her potential, she will step even further into her radiance. Your spouse will fill the space that he or she is given, whether it's in constant disappointment or unwavering belief.

To have someone see and acknowledge your best qualities ratchets up the level of intimacy in your relationship. It secures the bond. You're validated because your best qualities are recognized by the most important person in your life.

Become aware of your compliment-to-criticism ratio. Jon Butcher references this ratio in Lifebook, an intense personal-development program based in Chicago. I facilitated this program for four years and learned the importance of minding the compliment-to-criticism ratio. Of course, there's always going to be times when we have to criticize or bring forth a complaint, but if that's all you're doing, your marriage will suffer. Constant criticism erodes a marriage. The way to offset necessary criticism is to inject profuse levels of recognition and praise by creating opportunities to find the good in each other.

Myth: He Doesn't Need Another "Yes-Person" Around

In Chapter 2, we talked about how men need significance and women need security. In an entrepreneurial household, it's easy for a man to get his sense of significance from work because that's where he's engaging with his employees, customers, and advisors. Because he's in a position of leadership, it's likely that very few of these people tell him when he's falling short. If, at home, he's always receiving criticism, then, of course, he will spend more time at work. The home environment needs to be a place of refuge, safety, and significance for the entrepreneur, while providing a sense of security for the spouse. The fact that his spouse is likely to be the only one in a position to point out his weaknesses is yet another reason for her to also be one of his raving fans. It gives her more credence when she had to address his weaknesses.

More noteworthy is the realization that the entrepreneur may have a source of constant recognition from his business. Affirming staff, raving customers, and widespread publicity all speak to the accomplishments of the business owner. If the spouse does not work, she is likely not exposed to the same level of recognition or appreciation. In this case, it is CRUCIAL for the business owner to be mindful that he, alone, is her source of praise and encouragement. Expressions of gratitude will prove to be a game-changer for the spouse who has been feeling left in the shadows of success.

This is not limited to just compliments and criticisms—it also applies to our responses to success and failure. The degree of our reactions to positive news should exceed the degree of our reactions to negative news. When our spouse screws up, he or she knows it because we're throwing a fit. They know when they have messed up. Yet when they do well, we tend to take it for granted and don't celebrate it. The degree of celebration we have over successes should exceed the degree of disappointment we show in "failures." It's easy to be frustrated when the losses impact the family, but when things go well, it's crucial to celebrate the wins with the same vigor. Expressing frustration is easy. We often do it without even thinking about it. Because of this, it is imperative to build the muscle of appreciation to fortify the marriage.

Praise in Action

Begin paying attention to your compliment-to-criticism ratio by trying out these different strategies. Consider sitting down with a pen and sheet of paper and making two lists of all the criticisms and compliments you expressed in the last twenty-four-hours. Write down every single one you can remember, regardless of how significant or inconsequential it may seem. When you're finished, check to see which column is longer. Examine each line on your list. If the list of criticisms outnumbers the list of compliments, get to work on what you appreciate about your spouse. Work on that list until it exceeds the list of complaints. Seal the deal by sharing your newfound appreciation with your spouse.

Practice the art of the compliment. Giving compliments can generate positive perspective in oneself. Earlier in this chapter, I described how the same qualities can be seen as strengths or weaknesses, depending on our perspective and the context in which we view them. When you verbalize your appreciation rather than focus on complaints, it will cultivate your partner's traits as strengths and draw out more of his or her good, inspiring qualities. Isn't THAT the person you'd rather be married to anyway? Choose your view wisely, because it will determine who shows up for you.

Showing appreciation for each other in simple ways on a daily basis can contribute to building a powerful and long-lasting relationship. For instance, consider something as easy as leaving notes in a wallet or near the coffeepot. What if we could start the morning with a compliment?

Consider how it would feel to face every day with words of encouragement from your spouse. It could be like adding sweet sugar to your bitter coffee. Try this experiment: For one week, begin and end each day with a compliment to your spouse. Observe what changes, including how you and your partner feel about each other and your relationship.

The art of the compliment involves intentionality. It's about enacting and verbalizing your appreciation toward your spouse, rather than just taking his or her good qualities and successes for granted. Speak to your appreciation of what your partner is providing for you. Begin with his or her name, and then acknowledge a quality you normally don't recognize verbally; it can be a physical characteristic, an achievement, a personal quality, or a mind-set. Then share how it makes a difference in your life. You might say something like, "Renee, your intuition is always spot-on. Every time I honor your intuition, it saves me from so many headaches." Remember, acknowledge all the ways your partner contributes to the relationship: intellectually, emotionally, spiritually, socially, sexually, and/or financially. We want to become conscious of everything we are receiving and cultivate more of what is going well in our lives.

Praise can also be used as a mirror and a tool of accountability for when our spouse's strengths have turned into weaknesses. When you need to criticize, frame the statement in a way that is supportive and productive. Remember how a strength (like passion) can become distorted through a high-pressure situation and show up as a weakness (like anger). So when you want to be critical and blame, take a moment to reframe the statement as praise: "I can tell you're under a lot of pressure. You're at your best when you're creative and rested. Right now, this isn't you. How can we shift you back into your strength?"

Have an open attitude toward what you try, and keep in mind that these are just general recipes. The key concept is that there should be more compliments than criticisms in your relationship.

Find your partner's power phrase. When my superman, David, talks about losing his business in bankruptcy court, he mentions how it was my affirmations that kept him alive. I sent him emails and texts not only to validate him, but also to remind him of his ability, purpose, and greater vision. I loved David for who he was, and I believed in him. I saw his genius and nurtured his inherent strengths rather than reacting in panic to the external chaos he was experiencing. I recognized how there were specific and deliberate phrases that resonated with him: "I'm behind you all the way." "You've got this." "If anyone can do it, you can." Those platitudes sustained him in his darkest hours.

Discovering your own power phrase, as well as the power phrase of your partner, is crucial—but most people don't know what words will help encourage them and they don't know what their spouses need to hear. The power phrase is directly tied to our deepest fears. Verbally speaking out against these silent fears helps remind us of a more empowering truth, and that keeps us out of our caves of insecurity.

My deepest fear is that I'll screw up my kids. The power phrase I need to hear is this: "The way you see and nurture your children as individuals is empowering them to create their own extraordinary lives." I need to hear this from the person I am closest with, because it's an affirmation of how I can choose to believe in my vision instead of my insecurities and fear.

Fear is a vulnerable space we enter, one that is deeply intimate, and one where we must practice our greatest compassion and trust. To find your partner's power phrase, you must first discover his or her greatest insecurity and understand that this insecurity comes from fear. We can choose to support each other in the areas in which we are most vulnerable by speaking to our appreciation and cultivating steadfast belief, strength, and love.

I've worked with couples that, at the beginning of our coaching sessions, were not even aware of how much they were struggling. They were simply resigned to what their marriage had become and were going through the motions. When we began discussing their issues and these concepts behind praise, I watched as they took a moment to look at each other through a perspective of deep regard. With their relationships reinvigorated on the spot, and it was like they were seeing each other on their first day of marriage.

To love someone means to see them—all of them. It means to see them as their brightest, most alive and active self, and also to see them at their most vulnerable and insecure. When you love someone—when you can see them at their most basic, human level—you can appreciate what is most important to them. This is where love grows. This is how the bonds of a relationship strengthen.

To create your personalized action plan, visit:
www.playpraiseandpurpose.com

Chapter 6

THE POWER OF PURPOSE

A solo purpose divides; a shared purpose unites.

M ark Twain said, "The two most important days of your life are the day you are born and the day you find out why." If you've found your purpose, you know how much truth this quote holds. Discovering our purpose answers many of life's biggest questions: "What is the meaning of life?" "Why am I here?" "What is my genius?" And even, "Does my life matter?"

Colliding with purpose is one of the most exhilarating experiences we can have as a human being. Discovering our purpose not only changes the course of our lives, it also impacts the lives of everyone with whom we work. However, it can also come with a cost—particularly to a marriage. When we make the choice to turn our purpose into a profession, it can leave our spouse feeling like our work is more important than he or she is. If one spouse is purpose-driven and the other isn't, it can be especially hard to understand this relentless pursuit. The commitment to developing a shared purpose as a couple will help bring harmony to these entrepreneurial relationships.

I believe our individual purpose comes "factory installed" in us. It's an innate calling that, when tapped, becomes impossible to resist. As we pursue this purpose and the full expression of it, it can create a point of contention in our relationships. It can either leave our spouse feeling like our business gets the best of us while she gets the rest of us, or it can be a painful reminder that she has not connected with her own purpose yet. This chapter will serve as a guide for those couples experiencing the dark side of a purpose-driven life. We'll discuss how discovering our individual and shared purpose introduces us to who we are as our best and highest self.

Purpose Envy

My client Julie said it best: "I hate watching Jim walk out the door each day because he goes out to change so many lives and make a difference—and it's a daily reminder that I'm still searching." Like Julie, many spouses can feel a certain degree of envy that their entrepreneurial spouse has a strong sense of calling and meaning—while they don't. His sense of purpose, if not experienced by the spouse, can stir discontent or even resentment in a spouse. It can be difficult for a spouse to begin the pursuit of purpose in an entrepreneurial shadow.

It's natural for an entrepreneur to equate purpose to a business opportunity, but for a spouse who's not business-minded, that can be off-putting. The fact is, everyone has a purpose. It's a bonus to be paid for your purpose, but definitely not a necessity. You may be a whiz in the kitchen, or maybe you're made to be a parent or caretaker. Perhaps you're the one all your friends call for fashion advice or investment strategies. Purpose doesn't have to be translated into a business to make it valid. Purpose is anything that introduces us to our best selves. It's what motivates us to become better and better at something. It's what makes us stand up a little taller and hold our heads higher. It is the activity that helps us lose track of time and elicits that feeling of being delighted to be alive.

When Something is Missing, It's Probably Buried

I wholeheartedly believe that your purpose is already in you. I believe we each came into this life with a unique mission to impact the lives of our fellow humans. I also believe that at a young age, we have a sense of what this purpose might be. As we begin to express this to our friends and family, we are often shut down. Out of protection (love), our family might attempt to inform us of all the tragedy that we'll encounter if we journey into the pursuit of purpose. I sense this is changing as our human race evolves, but for Generation X and previous generations, there seems to be an experience of being told that we'll never make it if we reach for the stars.

For me, this was quite literal. I vividly remember the day my fourth-grade teacher announced we'd be doing a report on what we wanted to be when we grew up. We had just returned from the playground where I had spent the entire recess being chased in flirtatious pursuit by my classmate, Brian. With my newfound confidence, thanks to this blossoming crush, I was quick to volunteer my answer. I eagerly raised my hand and confidently proclaimed, "Mrs. Egezio, I'm going to be an astronaut!!" Without missing a beat ,my new crush—Brian—exclaimed "Kelly, you can't be an astronaut; you have to be *smart* to be an astronaut!"

The class erupted in laughter. And there it was. In that moment, I buried my dreams. In that moment, I chose to be the fun girl—the life of the party—so no one would laugh at my dreams again. As you'll remember, I even went to college and got a degree in "play." That provided me with even more fun as I landed jobs at Walt Disney World, Disney Cruise Line, and Hilton Head Island. What a great life, right?

But something was still missing. As you now know, I was missing my calling. Thankfully, I eventually found it, and through discovering that purpose, I learned to recognize the lie that I had created to keep myself safe from the rejection I experienced that day in fourth grade. If you find that you are in purpose-seeking mode, I challenge you to find the moment you decided to keep yourself safe. When did you decide that it was unsafe to pursue your dream? Go back to that moment. Can you see the lie? It is only in discovering the lie that we can reveal the truth.

When I realized I was basing my entire life around the faulty belief that my value as a person was to be fun, I was able to step more powerfully into my intelligence—and it changed everything.

Disparagement of our purpose is one of the harshest forms of criticism we can receive. In essence, we're being told we're not equipped to do what we are meant to do. Can you see how tempting it would be to shut down this pursuit altogether? The path of dogma can feel much safer than being told we're wrong about our own dreams.

This is where the quiet desperation sets in and that feeling that something is missing begins to arise. The moment you accept this calling and start saying *yes* to it is the moment your purpose will begin to reveal itself.

Letting Your Purpose Find You

Generally, the people I work with fall into two categories: purpose-driven or purpose-seeking. The truth is, most purpose-driven people I know didn't find their purpose; their purpose found *them*. And it happened by saying *yes* to something unexpected. This was true for me as well.

When I was twenty-five, I had just moved back to Chicago from Florida. I had no interest in finding my purpose because, quite frankly, I was still telling myself that I was supposed to be the fun one! I had big plans to get a job in special events because I figured that if I had to work, it might as well be at a party. I hired a headhunter to help me in my pursuit, and her first suggestion went over like a lead balloon. "I have a client called Strategic Coach. They set up workshops for entrepreneurs. I can get you an interview this week."

My knee-jerk reaction was, "No, way!" I imagined myself assembling trade show booths in sterile convention halls. "That's the last thing I want to do." But I needed a practice interview, so I begrudgingly told the headhunter to go ahead and schedule it.

I did no research on this company prior to my interview. I had no idea that coaching was an industry, or that this type of work even existed. But when I showed up at the offices of Strategic Coach in Rosemont, Illinois, I was captivated.

I call it my "mother ship" because the moment I walked in the door, I knew I wanted to be a part of this organization. The art on the wall, the books, and their mission ("Work Less. Make More.") all spoke to me. I was home.

As my interview began, I learned more about the concept of coaching entrepreneurs. It was so intuitive to me that I found myself "talking the talk" right away. That was the day everything changed for me. It was the first time I wanted more for myself. It was the first time I saw a bigger future for myself. It was the first time I met my higher self.

At long last, I started taking myself more seriously. I was no longer interested in just going out on the weekends and drinking margaritas. I wanted more for myself; I wanted to be around more inspiring people. I had realized that I could make a difference in people's lives, and that my own life—here—could actually matter. Before my interview, I hadn't been concerned with finding my purpose; now, I couldn't live without it. And it all started with an unexpected *yes*.

If you feel you are on the purpose-seeking end of the spectrum, congratulations! That tug is your indicator that you are on the brink. That void—or the feeling that there must be something more—is your calling to bigger things. However, I find that spouses of entrepreneurs tend to dismiss this feeling more than any other group. I hear things like, "We have such a great life; who am I to ask for more?"

And, "I feel bad about feeling unfulfilled; we have such an amazing life together. I don't know what's wrong with me." In my experience, I have found that spouses of entrepreneurs can get so caught up in the minutiae of everyone else's dreams and goals, they neglect their own. In this state, they get carried so far away from their personal desires that they end up getting squeezed out of their own lives. They look around at all they have and still feel like something is missing. That "something" is often their sense of self.

Moving from purpose-seeking to purpose-driven starts with giving yourself permission to ask for more. Accept that it's okay to seemingly have it all and still ask for more. That feeling *only* comes when there is more in store for you.

The Importance of a Shared Purpose

The power of purpose is more than an individual pursuit. It's *the* defining quality that takes couples from ordinary to extraordinary. Couples can be at odds over many things, including finances and parenting, but when they have a shared sense of purpose, they establish longevity and unity that surpasses their unaligned counterparts. The reason is simple: Purpose is fuel. It's the driving factor that allows us to plow through the obstacles to reach our goal.

One way to identify your purpose as a couple is to think about your life in five, ten, or fifty years. Whom have you helped? What is the difference you have made as a couple?

With whom are you spending time each day? For what reasons are people seeking your company? Your answers to these questions will help set the course for your direction as a purpose-driven couple.

Both partners are working toward the same goal, whether that's retiring on the beach, traveling 150 days a year, or starting a nonprofit. It can be to be totally focused on kids and grandkids, or to have the business carry on through future generations. The vision itself doesn't matter; what matters is that both the entrepreneur and his spouse share a powerful vision of where they are going *together*.

If a spouse has not experienced a personal sense of purpose, and is living with a purpose-driven entrepreneur, the first step is not necessarily to find her own life's purpose right away. Instead, it is to get on board with a sense of shared purpose in her relationship with her spouse. Both members of the couple can ask, "Where are we going together?" This question clarifies their expectations of their roles within the marriage. For example, if they share a retirement goal, what is the spouse doing to preserve the wealth? If it's a charity goal, which charity is it going to be and is the spouse contributing in other, nonfinancial ways? The object is for the entrepreneur and spouse to have a shared purpose in the relationship. Establishing purpose in the relationship helps to bring greater harmony and fulfillment to both parties.

Owning Your Brilliance
as the Gateway to Purpose

Jon Butcher, founder of Lifebook, and his wife, Missy, present a great example of how two extraordinary people can create that one extraordinary marriage through the power of purpose. After nearly thirty years together, they're the most legendary couple I've met, and among entrepreneurs, they're considered to be one of the most powerful couples in the community. It's no secret how they came to possess the sultry romance that they have: they have created a shared purpose that requires *both* of them to consistently show up as their best self in twelve categories of life.

Missy remembers how, when they first began dating, she held Jon in such high regard that she asked herself whom she had to be to become his partner. "I have to step up in every area of my life," she concluded.

Similarly, Jon has spoken about Missy, saying, "My love for her transcends my love of all else—my businesses, my children, everything! If I have to choose between work or being with Missy, it will be Missy every time because she's just such a magnificent creature." Missy is captivating to Jon because she's clear on her own purpose *and* has found the line between support and self-care.

Missy has owned her own brilliance. She felt that Jon was firing on all cylinders in so many areas of his life that she was inspired to elevate hers as well. She recognized that it takes *two* extraordinary people to create *one* extraordinary relationship. Looking at these two, they are an exact match (yet not a duplicate) in terms of how well they have elevated their respective games.

Entrepreneurs are wired to take extreme ownership over their lives. The spouse also needs to take ownership over her life, establish her own identity and activities, and pursue her own dreams and purpose. It is through this place of self-ownership and purpose that authentic growth will take the couple from ordinary to extraordinary.

Purpose in Action

Empowering the spouse to pursue her own goals and dreams, and to find a passion that revives her in her own unique way, renews the passion in a marriage. We focus on the spouse's personal life or her unique traits and gifts. Because our purpose lives in us, we strip away all the external factors—career, money, kids, spouses, parents, and other people's expectations. We focus on the six areas that make up her personal life and promote growth: energy, emotion, character, wellness and beauty, spirituality, and relationships. Understanding who she is *at her best* in these six categories is a powerful motivator for her to discover her greater purpose.

Energy. The most common objection I hear from spouses is there's no time to explore new passions. That's code for they are spending time (and energy) on all the wrong things. Before we can identify what we should start doing, we have to be clear on what to *stop* doing.

Everything in your life today served you at one point—that's why you did it. But to step into higher purpose, we need to rid ourselves of everything that no longer serves us. When we honestly look at our habits and see how much time we're spending on activities that add little value to our lives—like watching television or browsing social media—the results are shocking. There is especially enormous emotional baggage connected to social media; we see only the highlights of life, and that prompts us to compare ourselves to others. Managing or eliminating those habits creates more time and energy for bigger pursuits that are more aligned with where we want to go in life.

The exercise I referenced in Chapter 4, The Power of Play, is a powerful approach to creating energy for more fulfilling pursuits. In business, entrepreneurs often have a great deal of delegation power and are trained to focus on things at which they excel. In the household, a lot of the tasks entrepreneurs don't like to do get delegated to the spouse—but we want the spouse to adopt the same empowered mind-set of doing what energizes her and to delegate or eliminate the rest.

Of course, there are obligations we *have* to fulfill in our daily lives, like handling finances and feeding our kids.

Outsourcing activities that drain you and adopting strategies to better utilize time will open up the space and energy you need for the life you *do* want to have.

Thoughts & Emotion. If we aren't intentional about our purpose, we are at the mercy of external circumstances. Either we control our thoughts or our emotions control us. Work to identify and actively create the emotions you want to experience in your life. Start with what you're currently feeling. If your baseline emotional state is filled with anxiety, depression, or apathy, look at what's causing this stress and ascertain how you *do* want to feel. Ask yourself, "What do I need to do to create a space in which I am experiencing these positive emotions more often? With whom do I need to spend time? What places or activities will get me there? What thoughts and beliefs will create those emotions?"

Sometimes, it is only by becoming clear about your emotions that you can enact tangible change in your life. A client of mine, Gabrielle, had begun coaching while feeling unfulfilled, resentful, and uncertain. She often acted out in anger and was short-tempered and easily agitated. When issues arose in her life, she was apathetic and acted like they were everyone else's problem. When I asked her how she wanted to feel, she answered, "Fulfilled, at ease, passionate, and happy."

Through our sessions, we identified the source of her negativity: She *believed* everything in her life was falling short of her expectations. It was almost like she was hard-wired to find fault; she lived in constant disappointment of her husband, her kids, her house, and her career. By simply choosing more empowering thoughts that reflected the way she DID want to feel, she was able to live in greater joy and abundance.

Character. Who do you need to be to get everything you want? I used to think this was a manipulative question until I got to the core of what it really means: If you want a different result in your life, you have to start doing things differently. If you want to see direct, positive, and permanent changes in your life, you have to implement different daily habits on a cellular level, because that will change your character.

For example, I used to say that I wasn't an organized person; I just claimed it wasn't a part of my personality. Then I realized that if I wanted to grow a successful business, not being organized was holding me back. To get the result I wanted, I needed to retrain myself to maintain consistent records and keep my calendar in order; when I did this, organization became a part of who I am.

One character trait a lot of my clients work on is courage. This could mean the courage to get a babysitter and spend more time away from our kids, the courage to develop deeper intimacy with our spouse, the courage to go out and pursue that dream job, or even the courage to distance ourselves from friendships that are bringing us down.

Too often, we neglect our own wants and needs due to guilt narratives. We need to have the courage to believe that caring for and honoring ourselves first will produce positive results in every other aspect of our life. For instance, it is not easy for most women to be stay-at-home moms; I think women who can do that underestimate how important their work is. Women like Gabrielle and me—who love being moms but who are also driven to pursue dreams aside from motherhood—need to find the courage to release that guilt. Having a healthy attitude toward balancing family life with work life allows us to become happier and more fulfilled.

Wellness and Beauty. Our health is our first wealth. It is also the first data-point others use to determine how we expect to be treated. If we don't treat ourselves well, why should they?

When we look good, we feel good! Confidence is the electricity of life, so we must actively transform our outward appearances to reflect how we feel on the inside. It can be easy to "let yourself go" after marriage, but that lackluster external appearance will always translate to a dull inner light as well.

Through our appearances, we are also actively creating our own personal brands. For instance, when you choose clothing and accessories, do you have a style preference? Do you like to look sophisticated, or timeless, or original? What's the personal brand that resonates with you, that's always going to remind you to step into your best self in your work and with others?

The best beauty strategy is taking a proactive approach to maintaining your health—not waiting until you're sick to go to the doctor, but rather, preserving the state of well-being you already have. For me, that means chiropractic care, a balanced diet, massage, and enjoyable exercise. For you, it can include whichever healthcare and self-care rituals you maintain to preserve your well-being. It might involve practicing conscious eating—that is, slowing down to give your full attention to what and how much you're consuming. You might also want to stay active with exercise that you look forward to, like yoga, rowing, hiking, or running.

It's important to maintain our wellness and personal brand because this area touches every other area of our lives. When we start to neglect this area, it affects other areas of our lives, such as our self-esteem, our relationships, and even our finances. The maintenance of our health and appearance tends to be the last thing we let go of, and when we stop caring for ourselves, it's a primary indicator that we're near our rock bottom. It's also the first area we should focus on as we resume our climb back upward. It's THAT foundational.

Spirituality. We connect to spirituality when we ask the big questions like, "What is the meaning of life?" It's independent from religion, although for some people, spirituality and religion are entwined. Spirituality is connecting to our higher power, so for some people, that's God, or the Universe, or Source; others regard it as their own intuition. Spirituality is whatever life force guides you. It's where we can be still and hear that small voice inside us that helps us tap into our inherent knowledge.

To connect with your spirituality, the first thing to do is to clarify what this looks like for you. For some people, it means going to church, while for others, it's spending time in nature, or being by the water, or reading, or meditating. The important thing is to identify the rituals that will bring you closest to love and remind you of how you are part of a bigger picture. Connecting with your personal spirituality should inspire you to commit more energy to your exterior life by providing you a time of rest and reprieve.

Spirituality is the underlying connection between the six areas of growth. It's what gives us courage to go from being without purpose to purpose-seeking by saying yes to things we normally wouldn't say yes to. It's what helps us understand which negative activities and influences in life we can relinquish. As we identify our sacred rituals, we also understand what we must say no to in order to prioritize the practices that will most fully serve our life.

Relationships. It's important to surround yourself with people who challenge you to improve and who support your goals and dreams. As motivational speaker Jim Rohn once said, "You are the average of the five people you spend the most time with." You want to have relationships with people who are working to better themselves. When the sky's the limit, everyone elevates one another.

Our identities are often fed by the people with whom we spend the most time. If your social network is mostly made up of negative people, it will be much harder for you to keep up your motivation and grow. Often, when people begin the pursuit of purpose, the people around them begin to feel threatened. Their friends may think, *Wait a minute; if she starts to grow, she may outgrow me.* They may work to keep you in *their* comfort zone by projecting fear and negativity. They may be unsupportive or show signs of jealousy or that oh-so-supportive pretense of protection: urging you to "just be happy with what you've got."

The art of letting go is useful here. There is a common, emotionally charged perception that women have a fixed group of friends they are supposed to maintain relationships with throughout their lives. But the truth is that our social circles are always evolving. Our connections are transient. If you look at your current social circle, you'll notice that it includes people from every phase of your life, from your work friends to your church friends to your old college friends to the friends you see at your kids' sports games. You're already connected with many different groups, and social circles change and evolve quickly these days. If you are spending a lot of time with old childhood friends and are looking for a more encouraging group, you can start to shift more of your attention to your friends from the gym, work, or school. Give yourself permission to move on and find a more positive social network; it might be easier than you think.

In Summary

Focusing on these six areas of personal development will empower you to see yourself in your highest light and break the chains of an unfulfilling life. Who are you as your highest self in each of these categories? More important, what becomes possible for you when you are clear and confident in each of these areas? All the things you desire in life—deeper relationships, wealth generation and preservation, leaving a legacy, making a difference, serving others, purchasing your dream home, maintaining solid business growth—are the *result* of the work you will do in these six crucial areas. Once you are clear on that, you can change the game for yourself and your family.

To create your personalized action plan, visit:
www.playpraiseandpurpose.com

THE LAUNCH PAD:
IT TAKES TWO EXTRAORDINARY PEOPLE TO CREATE ONE EXTRAORDINARY RELATIONSHIP

Being an entrepreneur can be a long, lonely road. This gives rise to the need for coaches and mastermind groups. When entrepreneurs find opportunities to connect with others going through the same manic journey, it alleviates the self-doubt and feelings of being overwhelmed that we experience when we're in isolation.

Until now, spouses have not had that luxury. Spouse programs have been offered as a vehicle to encourage spouses to become an even stronger support system to their entrepreneurial husband or wife. I believe this widens the divide between a purpose-driven entrepreneur and his or her spouse. This misses the transformational aspect of developing a shared purpose in our most intimate relationship.

When the entrepreneur and his or her spouse are focused on becoming the best versions of themselves, they become more resilient to the added stress entrepreneurship brings. The entrepreneur can only go so far in business without the support of his or her spouse. Conversely, the spouse can only expand as far as she can envision herself going. In order for both of them to reach their fullest potential, both parties need to be actively engaged in the creation of their joy and fulfillment through play, praise, and purpose.

Linda, a former client, watched her life unfold in unexpected ways after she connected to her own sense of purpose. Linda and I met when her husband, Chris, was looking for coaching for his own career transition. Chris was a newly retired NFL player complete with a Super Bowl ring. His identity was tied strongly to being a pro athlete, and he was searching for his next step. As Linda listened to our conversation, she began to ask herself the same question: "What's next for me?"

Over our weekend together, she entertained the idea of going back to the design career she'd had before her first child was born. But that didn't ignite her in the way she was hoping; she still wanted more. While searching for her next step, an opportunity presented itself that, ordinarily, she would have emphatically dismissed. Linda's friend told her about a new, all-natural cosmetic line that was available for direct sales. Selling beauty products was definitely not on Linda's radar, but how could she say no to a new opportunity when she had spent weeks praying for a new opportunity? Surprisingly, she went for it and launched her own Beautycounter business. She became engaged with and excited about this industry-changing product, and her business took off! By her second year, she took the stage at the company's national conference as one of the top producers. She spoke in front of thousands of women about the power of saying yes! She later confided in me that she had always harbored a secret envy of her husband's commitment to, and passion for, his work. Experiencing that passion for herself changed the game in their relationship. She had finally experienced the power behind finding her purpose.

Discovering her purpose not only changed her life, it also changed her marriage. It opened up an entirely new avenue of communication with her husband that she had never experienced before. It gave them a new shared language as they connected over individual passions. That deepened their intimacy, because they now saw the absolute best in each other. What had been just a strong marriage became a passion-driven love affair built on mutual respect and adoration.

The Powers of Play, Praise, and Purpose

If the goal in business is to scale *up*, the goal in marriage should be to scale *together*. This often happens by getting back to the basics. **The most extraordinary couples share**

a common purpose, and the focus of my program, and this book, is to coach couples through the three P's: Play, Praise, and Purpose.

The power of play is how spouses reconnect to each other and remember why they fell in love in the first place. Through play, they dissolve tension and share a united pursuit of enjoyment. Play is where our greatest strengths are revealed and how we remember not to take ourselves so seriously.

The power of praise is a reminder that our greatest strengths are always our greatest weaknesses. Focusing on strengths more often than we point out weaknesses keeps secure the admiration, respect, and love in a relationship. When we become conscious of our compliment-to-criticism ratio, we can focus on praise to acknowledge and encourage the positive qualities in our partners.

The power of purpose focuses on couples establishing their shared, long-term vision. While many entrepreneurs derive their sense of fulfillment from the business, it's important for them to also feel purposeful in their marriage, so both partners gravitate toward the relationship as a foundational source of love and provision.

When spouses find a passion that is unique to them as individuals, it translates to a sense of shared purpose as a couple. Focusing on the spouse's personal life to work through the six categories of growth—energy, emotion, character, wellness and beauty, spirituality, and relationships—helps identify that purpose. These categories also help entrepreneurs grow their business by investing in the foundation that is their marriage.

We are most alive when we are in love. To experience the absolute best this life has to offer, you must fully recognize and understand this one simple fact. You have *everything* you need *right now* to create the most extraordinary love relationship your mind can comprehend. Show up as your *best* for your spouse. You have tremendous qualities to offer your partner. You bring to the table a bounty of traits, talents, and relationships that enrich your life together. When you fully step into that brilliance, you extend a loving and irresistible invitation for your spouse or partner to do the same. When the two of you accept the calling to show up as your best for each other, you will have mastered the single greatest relationship secret: it takes **two** extraordinary people to create **one** extraordinary relationship.

ADDITIONAL INFORMATION

Renewing Yourself through Your Marriage

While couples may go to counseling to resolve a past hurt, the focus of coaching is building a powerful future. There are countless executive coaches and mastermind groups that focus on the entrepreneur's leadership abilities and business acumen, but no one is addressing the real opportunity that lies in the power of the spouse. The spouse represents half of the entrepreneur's success, and it's important for entrepreneurs to take the same ownership in their marriage as they do in their businesses.

Business coaching has proven invaluable to millions of entrepreneurs around the world as they grow their businesses. Unfortunately, business growth can drive a psychological wedge between spouses. It is critical to grow your relationship as steadily as you grow your business.

The simple, daily strategies that allowed you to develop your love as a couple in your dating days are the same strategies that will allow you to flourish as a couple. It takes two extraordinary people to create one extraordinary life. Welcome to your most extraordinary life!

Entreprenewer Coaching Services

My coaching method begins with a couples-coaching call based around the Kolbe profile. The Kolbe offers practical insight into one's instincts, which gives language and awareness to how each person gets his or her best results. It's a non-confrontational conversation that makes light of the mania that often exists in entrepreneurial households. Once both parties have a thorough understanding of each other's unique talents, they may opt-in for more in-depth coaching in the Entreprenewer program. This program is a six-session coaching intensive that allows participants to strip away the residue of guilt and obligation and step into who they are at their best. We hear a lot of talk about becoming "the best version" of ourselves—but what does that really mean? Meditating more? Working out more? Volunteering more? Maybe, but the Entreprenewer program will reveal your highest self in the six most crucial areas of identity. This can take place in a private series, a group series (open to the public), or a closed group (available to existing groups or masterminds).

I've watched "ordinary" people create extraordinary relationships by aligning through play, praise, and purpose. They learn to prioritize themselves—and then their marriage, as the foundation of their relationship. In doing so, they are able to develop a strong, unconditional bond that strengthens them as individuals along with their families and businesses. We've rewritten the rules of business. It's time to rewrite our rules of marriage.

Learn more about Entreprenewer coaching services at: www.playpraiseandpurpose.com

NOTES

NOTES

NOTES

NOTES

NOTES

NOTES